Two Horse Wagon
Going By

BY THE SAME AUTHOR

Torse 3: poems 1949–61 (1962)
Nonsequences / Selfpoems (1965)
Our Flowers & Nice Bones (1969)
The Lonely Suppers of W.V. Balloon (Carcanet, 1975)
Pataxanadu and Other Prose (Carcanet, 1977)
Carminalenia (Carcanet, 1980)
111 Poems (Carcanet, 1983)
Serpentine (Oasis Books, 1985)

CRITICISM

'Bolshevism in Art' and Other Expository Writings
   (Carcanet, 1978)
The Pursuit of the Kingfisher (Carcanet, 1983)

TRANSLATIONS (select)

Modern German Poetry 1910–60
   (with Michael Hamburger, 1962)
Friedrich Nietzsche, *Selected Letters* (1969)
Robert Walser, *Jakob von Gunten* (1969: 1983)
Friedrich Hölderlin and Eduard Mörike, *Selected Poems*
   (1972)
Elias Canetti, *Kafka's Other Trial* (1974)
Robert Walser, *Selected Stories* (1982)
Goethe, *Selected Poems* (1983)
Gert Hofmann, *The Spectacle at the Tower* (1985)

CHRISTOPHER MIDDLETON

Two Horse Wagon Going By

CARCANET

ACKNOWLEDGEMENTS

Grateful acknowledgement is made to the periodicals in which some of these poems first appeared:
Aileron, Grosseteste Review, New Orleans Review, Ninth Decade, Perception, Poetry Australia, Poetry Nation Review, Richmond Arts (Virginia), *Sulfur, Verse.* Some other poems appeared in the last section of *111 Poems* (1983).
'Woden Dog' first appeared in book form in a limited edition handset by Rosmarie and Keith Waldrop of Burning Deck Press, Providence, Rhode Island. Some details in 'Wild Flowers' are taken from Loren Eiseley's book *The Immense Journey*.
I also owe thanks to the D.A.A.D. Artists Program for the opportunity to spend several months in Berlin in 1978.

Published in 1986 by
Carcanet Press Limited
208–212 Corn Exchange Buildings
Manchester M4 3BQ, UK
and 108 East 31st Street, New York, NY 10016, USA

British Library Cataloguing in Publication Data
Middleton, Christopher, 1926-
Two horse wagon going by
I. Title
821'.914   PR6025.I25

ISBN 0–85635–661–1

The Publisher acknowledges the financial assistance of the Arts Council of Great Britain

Cover photograph: fragment from Tun Huang, 9th/10th century A.D. Reproduced from William Cohn, *Chinese Painting*, 2nd edn, 1951.

Printed in England by SRP Ltd, Exeter
Typeset by Dentset, Oxford

Contents

Silent Rooms in Several Places

Apocrypha Texana

1

2

3

"A wagon went by. Two horses were in front of it, and on its high seat was a man with his hat on sideways and a woman with a big fascinator hiding her face. There was seven children in the wagon — two with sleeps upon them and a little girl with a tam-o'-shanter and a frown and a cape on her. I have thinks from the looks on their faces they all did have wants to get soon to where they were going to."

Opal Whitely, *The Story of Opal* (1920)

Silent Rooms in Several Places

1

Old Water Jar

Like one of the old ideas
It won't hold water any more
But it is round in the belly
And has strong bladed
Shoulders like a good woman
Elegant even the curves
Run down from the mouth
In a long sweet wave
You can't help liking it so
Simply for the way
It stands there

Suddenly Remembering You Still, Cecile

No such owl
Might exist, who said I saw it,
Silhouetted against
A tangle of
Chimney pots and starlit

Down it swoops, the wings
Curve like shark fins up from its
Ocean
Blue body, for, having never
Flown so far

Out of sight, it clove
Through towers of whispering thistle,
Midnight potato garden,
Sensed a military
Silver button

To be pelts of mice, but
Has revived, peat
Vapour bubbled from the throat
Of an ancient whisky jar,
And now has heard them,

Now it hears them,
Lips,
Wrinkled lips of an old woman,
Insomniac, beautiful
Still, breathing

Jacob's Hat

The great boled oaks lift up their limbs
To paint the air

But Jacob's water bottle and his cloak
Are heaped beneath his hat

And the sheep and the shepherd on horseback
Have somewhere else to go

Is it not curious, Jacob's hat?
The crown is tall, of straw, the broad brim

Crumpled like the edge of a mushroom
No, the top lip of a madman

Take your eye off it if you can
To watch Jacob's knee

Ram the groin of the angel or gather
The muscle tension

Making a shadowy ocean of
The flesh on his back

You do not hear the sheep bleat
Or the river ripple

You do not choke on the dust kicked up
By the shepherd's horse

You might not even notice the painting oaks
Or the spear laid across

Jacob's bundle of belongings, or the sword
Dropped in its sheath

Only the hat absorbs the shock of attention
An old straw hat

For all the world like a skull fungus
Doffed evidently by Jacob

Who took time enough to put in order
His precious few belongings

And with his well worn hat crown the heap
Before he sprang at the angel

Eight Skips around the Aura of Erato

1

These things that trouble us — on a bench
Under trees, talking: Where to start?
The heat and
The boats going out and
Thunder cracking across the sky and
However tenderly you held my hand it didn't mean

What I made of it. Contacts
Break down. The old absorbent aquifer
Common sense, who has it?
Who can guarantee anything?

2

Signed, a picture of you,
Dangerous. It has to touch
The sky, this feeling, keen, it

Hurts (and the rest —
Routine, buckling down, the "norms") but here
You help me to imagine one "flesh," sliced

And falling open, reformed, in our airy
Intermittent sort of time: "gods" — would they
Sense across their knuckles

Our whole dance, how it tugs at their strings?

3

Running, scared, because it
Makes no sense? No, this time no fear. Not
Even longings

Vague as with age bodily the blue
Fades in dragonflies. Watch, I'll cook for you
This crock of wine. We make peace,

Peace, of a kind.

4

Those bluegray harmless doves
Haunting your head

Fly out and in, imploring

I fumble through my clothes for their target
Find later the beak marks

They stripped off my skin

5

Never once a chance, or no, once only,
To look up and — all right, beep-beep,
Probably they were there, blinking

So it was for them
You said: I'm being born; and I heard, as never,
Space come home to the shape of a tune

6

Shadowy alley aflutter with birds
Small café, green with spinach
Somehow nobility when you say nothing

I must not wither this by thought
Nor cramp it into corners made in air
By speech. You hoard the cryptic leaf
And tree, fish, herb, one day to make

Out of their scattering one more image to live by

7

These things that trouble us:
There it is, the mansion, imagine, the orthodox
Statues bathed between fountains. We'll walk
That way, foreigners, into the cool, wondering;
It is dawn, nobody else hears
In that suspense the heaven bird warble.

Soon, soon
Little old women, worried in silent rooms,
Make shopping lists and correct the angles
Of their hats. Poof! The wind has warped
The forgotten sock a widow still is darning . . .

　　　　　　　8
Molds, grown over us. Scrape
Them off. Let your keel, solo, cut
Through the bustling
Adverse waters.

　　　　　　　Sing. From where I am
I'll hear it flutter, let me
See my skin
Stream from your masthead, hang it there.

Shih-Ch'u's Magic Letter

On Footpath Mountain
Once I stayed as a guest;
Poems, brush, even now
Mountain colour drenches them.
Thirty years you've been there;
They fondle bones of rock,
Unfancy words of yours, I think.

Steam of cloud and water rises
Here, at Hsi-ch'eng.
Midges flit, intrepid, each
Quick as a painted hawk.
Your Buddhist cell, so help me,
I envy it, your snow cold —
In long glowing lamps
Motionless orchid oil.

I have arrived, look now,
Friends on the mountain know it;
What sort of a state I'm in,
All run over to see:
Calumniated as I am,
Worse off by far than others,
I have two eyes intact,
Can still write tiny characters.

Iphigenia Ingénue

Whole streets of new trees now she'll suppose
Carry themselves so lightly; dogwood —
Radiant branches
Lift no stranger fruit than waxy
Pink petals

Entirely opening their bodies to the light
Slow substances have ringed the earth
For any plum to splash
A burning white up. Those violet fleets compose
A sky, their cool discrepant
Fragrance melts
Boneheaded categories

What is this secret haunts the earth
To curb oppression? It is hers: kept
Dark in her silver box —
A flower, crisp, and a carnelian moon,
Two feathers touching brush her cares away

Also an involved sea shell she keeps
In her silver box, at least
So she says, but
That's about all — my voice
Escapes for singing and my eyes you said
Go misty when you say a thing to excite me, sad
Or happy

In Anatolia

Slit eye, so young, in your place,
I mean no harm, but see you
And am close, in this light, so
Close. Food, knives, a red floor peak
And are gone in your flesh glow. The curve
Of a bird comes back to me.

Yes, it was big, as birds go. Blue wings,
A throat, I think, rain-rose, and a crest.
All at once it flew out of no place.
It perched on a plinth of white stone
To flute the one song it knew.

Noon: heat in this old town spent
Long breaths on rock. Wells dry. A few
Cubes of shade. Candid weeds made sure
The song could last. Pure notes
Go well with dust; in the doom of that high place
Time showed its drift.

On that plinth it put down claws, a bird,
Spikes — it told the air
What it meant: *io dio*, it sang. *Io dio*.
You will not say it. Your hair is
Coiffed to fall, soft, across your face,
As if your face should not be shown here —

A wing, gloss, when
You shake your head like that you hide
Most, at least, of your face. Wax
Boys, they sit, one by one, dumb, with hands
They fold and twist, here, at this feast:
You do not foot their bill.

Rich you might be, or
Not, but are you here? Your place seems
Close to oak boards, wild rice, raw fish.

That blue bird, you are with it.
Still you have ways to resist
Dead mouths, our small norms, blood that froze,

So much heart ache. Why, white stones
Once were grooved, to hold up roofs. White
Stone, fierce hands hewed it
Into forms. Through the fresh
Stone robes a god flew, those days, a pulse
It was thought. Worse off by far,
We have none or put ours in the wrong place.

Stand there and speak. Tell
Why no springs flow there. Why no folks walk
The old streets. Did the no-good bird
Eat the gods up? Let your wing fall
To hide your face. We do not know
What now to fear most.

Pink Slippers

Pink slippers —
The voices
Return, the voices
From Antioch, Agrigentum, wherever
Return, clear

Splitting apart
The bottled, rotten
Remnant we
Dwell in, with a swish
Of clothes falling

From limbs radiant
The voices
Return. She stood
And shook
Off everything, stood

In the silver light
A moment,
In a forest, in
A city, ancient lamps
Marble paving —

And the pink
Slippers? Later they
Crossed
A road, other feet
Than hers in them,

But to death
He loved them. Pink
And voices, distinctly
They spoke, delivering the drift
Of old stories —

Wickedly
The swish, the dark
And silver joy, the arms
Holding, the perfect
Fit, immediate

22.XI.84 In Memory of Julius Bissier

FOR JOHN ASH

A happy skill, when first light strikes
Home on the peak —

Snowy, the light, a moment
Only, it came with horse hair,

A pernambuco bow.
Counting out the practice

Years it took, now a breath
So singular, off it floats

Parting branches, for a glimpse
Of heaven in the air

Eccentricities of Diet

Aha, cloud, a cauliflower
        and us to eat it.
But soon, off this
        groaning table,
We'll suck and gnaw our
        neighbour's house,
Ripe, a cheese — thatched
        Norwegian Tilsit.

Seconds after, ask the sky:
        was this duplicate
Food a trick of guilt? Feed
        your face. Refreshed,
Weight expels the cacky
        cumulus of bishop,
Cat, whiplash, phosphorous
        rot from your crypt.
Still from hand to mouth,
        still it bloats
The vault — a perpetuity
        none care to live.

How soon gone, finwinged
        fork, your silver
Beauty glinted! What if she
        and her knife hear
Our teeth grind against bare
        unplotted bones? No
Way goes back, in. We have to
        bite like the blazes,
Hard, bite off clean
        their stainless heads.

Another Village

— Atmosphere
Wrong: past noon a sunlight
Denser than flesh, across
A bowl of red

Berries women at the
Marbletop
Table
Softly talking —

And the wild, fingery
Garlic flanks
The ravine, apricots
Quicken to be bitten —

Old bell, one chime
Remote — wind down deeper
Ruffling vine leaves;
Muscular,

Gorged with heat
A pine cone prepares
To open, crack, the poplar
Shivering — bluer, there

And now a mountain
Lifts, the idiot
Framing a theme can
Sit up and write about it

Exercise for a Singer

1

Certain songs —
Forests of light —
Belong to gods. Others propose
A shape of knowing. These retain
What comes from them.

2

Yours, the songs
You make your own, are framed
Likewise: by fictions.
      Heavenbent
You quarry from the earth a curling sign
For joy, for despair,
With luck, a home.

3

You are
A cave. First a mouth. Then
A throat. Shallow breath in it. Not
So fast. Breathe deeper, roll
The hollow around.

     It is filling
Your nostrils now, yours. Blow out the random
Unwanted air. The cave begins
To glisten. Silver snow,
       Folds of fire, it is
Luminous, heart,
Now lungs, the cave is belly, sex, contract
Muscle to feel it.

4

The cave, a rose, in
Or out of you, is opening, large.

Larger still, like time before,
Time after you. No song in that time.

Only a sign, hollow, your body, universe:
A big clay pot in the making, on a wheel.

The wheel, you make it spin. The wheel
Darkness. Of earth now
No thought, no china
Crashing to the floor, no canopy
For heaven. Signs.

The cave is enormous with breathing.
See this bird come to live in it.

5

A bird, many coloured. Plumage
Glows in a perfume
You dash on air, fling through dark
Like a wave with its rainbow. Thumb pressed
On a latch, you pushed an old gate open:

6

Summer garden, flowers, many
Names near-forgotten. The bird is chamairis,
Wild strawberry, quadlin, in leaf
A white thorn, dammasin, quince;
Germander, the bird, bear's foot,
Monk's hood and water mint

The bird, it is musk rose, later in August
Melocotones, also musk melon,
But unattached
Always it dwells, the bird, in the fountain form
Shaping the cave. Walkways, galleries
Harbour its orderly manifold in a shimmer.

7

At home in the hollows, feel
The bird's delicate bone cathedral around you:
Flute bones,
Breast and shoulder bones, legbones
Tunnelled — conch, trumpet,

Hummingbird feather: passages,
In them the air is you. All of you
Rushing through feathery hollow silence.

8

When the bird flies out, at dusk, be ready.
Nothing tense, no
Effort. Spread (and hang there, lightly
From your eyebrows) finger and toe. Likely as not

The closeness of
Everything will stun the bird —
If it flew. Now, now
Or never, with one breath disperse
Clustered faces
To the boundaries of your universal hollow. Four
Walls cannot object, nor anxious
Roofs, abolished clouds.

9

Now fresh clouds and stars are in their places.
Demons, too, you put them in their places.

These
Bodies all compose a ring, singular
Each, with longing, each remote.

10

Never or now
A song pretends to sing. You
Take your time. You made the space for it
To be given. Still it is little,
It is calling. It needs to be invented. Now
You take it up. You sing.

One for the Birds

Fact is, a soul at fifty comes unstuck.
Fiery flakes of it haunt a magnolia tree,
Haunt it, not the sootless way
Square but derelict lots of me
Perceive it.

Ghostly sputterings touch
Close to the crest. Then roots run out
Licketysplit and hobble me.
Am I the matter of my doubt,
A joke apart, glued to my tree?

Ivory blooms, undaunted, one flesh,
Dry as they look, bathe in all
The popular damps that entangle me.
A sweat of terror breaks my fall,
Upward, out of the psychocrypt.

Fabled scavengers, make room,
You turkey buzzards inking out the skies,
Avert your crotchety stare, if you can,
Save me a vastness in mid-air
To fuel my eyes.

Unfold, rainbow. Never enough. Some fifth
Element, neither a clod nor an empire
To float a gaze or steady a hand,
How will it beckon home, into the open,
A star stuff all other acts have orphaned?

Pleasure of a Consonance

At Issy-L'Evêque distinctly
Nesting in pine crests
Chimneypots and pointy turrets
Of a rose château

The Shape

Funny, you keep it to yourself. Not quite:
Scraps of the story escape, take on
A runaway life of their own. Funny
It has to hurt so, hurt so, still.
Draw breath, deep, breathe again, if you can.

Waking in a blinded room, improvising a vision
For her: dawn breaks over a brigantine,
From Patras to Palermo. Listen to the sea.
Mystery Greeks, bottles of ouzo, scent of pine.
This wheeze (it has to be) of an accordion.

Or worshipping one curl, all of a piece with her.
Had anyone noticed it? No, nobody before.
One touch and the cusp unfurls to cling
Close to an ear. It had to mean no less than love,
Perfect in sunlight, more than one half-afternoon.

Now it's nothing, nothing at all, she says.
Drunk as owls the sailors dropped asleep.
What is that faint plume on the horizon,
Not even marking the repeatable sea?
The curl persists, another where the lips

Of her sex meet. But she took off, that was it.
Forest thickens, torn you roll in it alone.
The room, sunken, waits for an oak to grow,
Fresh planks, to house again the shape
That shelters what escapes for it is certain.

To Draw the Bow at a Venture

It is necessary to brush the gold on silk
Necessary to remove all objects from the table
To put the dish back on its shelf
And the book, the cup, the banana,
The memories back into their cloudlikeness

It is not necessary in the least
But it is necessary to melt the walls
With their bricks and pictures
Necessary to take an axe to the door
And smash it open, the roof also

It is necessary to tell everyone go away
Leaving your presences only
Your presences which in a moment of thought
Bend this mind with a shock and set it free
To look at you without presumption

Then it is necessary to pluck out of vacancy
The bristles of word
And fit them into the holes of syntax
Necessary to school the worms of speech sound
And let them weave a lingo fabric

It is not necessary when the brush
Offers itself to the fingers immediately
And the fabric is a form born already among the chance
    tunes
Among the ghosts that laugh below the clashing textures
Some still fondly call a human mind

It is necessary that the form be born
As it were involuntarily in a single moment
It is necessary also that the silk be untorn
That the brush be ready for any surprise
That the holes be eager and glistening

Then it is necessary to dismantle what you did
Necessary to scrap the whole thing and start over
It is not necessary to worry about the thing
To be born in joy is all it asks for
Real tensions have to thrum in all the hairs and worms

It is not necessary any more
And no such thing is ever simply given
It is necessary to pick up hairs and worms and holes
And scatter them around the indelible space
Which speaks with walls and doors and presences

It is necessary to pull the room into place again
Simple and open to the old and new times
Situated on silk
Inflicting the normal horror on no-one
A cup, a dish, a book for once on the table

Not necessary — weightless

Relic

Powdered wood from a beam
And plaster from the ceiling
Sift into dunes among the random
Worm-holes peppering my desk.

Overhead the flying machines
Buzz, on their occasions. I admire
The hood worn by the lime tree;
Scent of its flowers, I breathe it in.

They cluster in threes or fours, like bells;
Bees in the hood and scarabs hum;
The bird with a black mask stops to listen,
Spidery claw on a flagstone.

I am wondering at the fluency of its lines,
And how the tail flits, when all at once,
At the top of the winding stair,
You stand in a torrent of light,

Dressed in silver linen, as you wave,
Hatless, ready to go, your sleeve
Uncaptured, a spray of flower bells
Tilting across the tassel of your parasol.

2

Rilke's Feet

1

Heart bowels hand head and O the breast
So many of the parts fan out
Pressing on speech
Each a shape distinct
At length delivered a message
Classified sensitive

2

Perched in my tree as the light
Tries to unfold over Wilmersdorf

Rilke's feet a phrase
Ran amok in the mass below —

But in the grass
Not a trace left — playing

Woodland god he walked there
Barefoot — before architecture

Boiled the green to stone gray—
1897: I had taken my shoes off . . .

3

Sweetheart, Lou

. . . what is God, Mama?

            "White hinds
        hidden in a thorn thicket"

No compliment to the long
Undulant chevelure of Magdalen

On a billow of mud
        in the Dordogne or Ariège was it
A footmark printed
        lightly
Hard mud in a deep cave

Might last another 15,000 years

But Rilke's feet
        he left them
                standing
To be invented

4

This hot pursuant of
The Incomparable

A sort of hassock stool
He kept and kneeling on

Upholstered velvet
Worshipped any woman

He had invited no
Not any but this

Was the way he tended
Kneeling on the stool

And gazing up as
She waved an arm or

Cringed and bit her lip
Footless for some quaint

Antiphallocratic reason he
Poised at hers

A projectile
In a catapult

5

Or Rilke had no feet at all
What he had was fins
Up he twiddles into the air

Sycamore seed going the wrong way
Lands in my tree
Owl's eyes large liquid

Blink at me   Contrariwise
He had no body just a head
Thought a little girl

No body in his clean but threadbare
Clothes crossed the room
And took a cake with Mama later

Off again
Somehow bowing
Where can he have put that cake

6

More famous feet
Than these invisible ones
The foot of Philoctet-
Es and Byron's

Hoof with its iambic knock
On the deck of a gondola,
Incidentally — copper,
His horse adored the hot

Weight of it and ladies
Lifted fingers to their eyes,
Thrilling stomachs
Fancy the surprise

Suddenly milord is dead
While muttering Greek
Bandits around his bed
Frenetically seek

To screw the damn thing off,
Here's Philoctetes' foot
Festering in a cave —
His wound minute by minute

Throbs away the years
Four thousand of them spin
Till Troy falls to hexameters
And Rilke's feet begin

7

A Wicked One
When he scraped the Many
Bits together
Must have made some funny faces

Rilke's feet — how
Is this body
To be looked upon: a

Screen or
Not sure a
Scene a recipient interim

And liminally
In and over it creation's
Wavering shapes break open
Yet

Are distorted it is
The dance but done
As if by hangmen

Touch and look
From a footsole run
Tightrope lines to every single organ

8

Voice where are you now
Tree what has become of you
Never a column or pedestal

But a tree of branching blood vessels
A tree trying to speak
Through thunderous pumping of juices
I climb across this voice
In the grip of its twig deletions

9

Hands whose touch is thinking
        How the taste of orange flows
To the beat of a ringdance

Slowly out of its givens
        The automatic body
Builds itself

Might balance feet with
        Strong straight
Articulations but dammit

An orchestra of echoes
      Code of interchanging
Trait and ancestor

All we can see in one photo
      Is Rilke in
Well shone shoes with spats

Its constant monologue
      Broken by torture
Reroutes no signals

And a shoe might hide
      One discord perhaps a hand
Froze an insurgent impulse

And clogs
      In the negative
I am told

Now like an undesired
      Eyeball captive in a pod of skin
For fingers wished it

Footward as a pipesmoker
      Tamps tobacco
Down to the base of the pipe bowl

So blue huggermugger knobs
      When bones obtrude strum on tendons
Fuming toes

Recoil to plot
      Inversion of the message
Train to be fingers and pluck back

Their slice of the power
      Did Rilke then support a claw
Brain-limb feedback

Did it flush his touch of sphinx
        Faintly at the tip
With repression's rose

10

Rilke's feet
Wading in a weird
Kettle of fish

        The lobster
Has gone for a walk
With his ghost
The sea
Once
Too often

11

Xenophon Xenophon it were fit to include
Dark as it is again in Wilmersdorf
An echo of your script from Corinth, your
Fictional grammar of the human foot

Anabasis uh I am tired and my secret
Reader wonders where we have got
As did your mob of Greeks thirty years before
Thirty years before you finally wrote

A bit boastfully about the march to the sea
Then how your lines inch by inch
Barrelled along the barbarous coast

But hardly anyone cares now
About the fleetfooted Carduchi
Peltists and bowmen coming up quick

When they shoot they put the left foot
Out and rest the base of the bow on it
Drawing back the string

You must have stopped to see that

And soon backwards the snow
Is opening its white tomb

Illshod columns of infantry
Straggle into Armenian mountains
Was there no shit they could not bite through

Newly flayed oxenskin
Froze that night to the footsoles
Thongs cut into ankle flesh

Many perished
Snowblind thwacking spear on shield
Throat racket body racket made the foe
Feel outnumbered

Small bags later we tied
To the horse hoofs else
In the snow to their bellies they sank

12

Can I speak to you now Rilke
As we sleep
A little for our lives
Though I wonder sometimes what you meant
And my memory is awful
The footless motions you enact or track

In poems where the verbs
Amaze by their precision
Were you pointing
Beyond the combative body which engulfs
All as nothing with its bubble

Pointing to a body more like music
A luminous relator with its warmth
"Transfiguring the earth"
If it was this what have we got
Not evil quite wondrous desires
But injustice

It may be too late
Your invisible
Feet can do nothing but insist
Issue into a space all
Rondure and volume void

Of anything more dense
Than the thrum of air you felt
Around a seagull's wing
As it poured the pearliness in
And fitted feathers

Threadless motion
Through it your truant feet
Sprinkling punctures might
Sustain
Like intervals between them utterly

Determined throngs of stars
Or freely quickening and distinct
These feet it is
That ease
The gasps of joy from children's throats

3

Quasizeros

21 MISCELLANEOUS MICRO-POEMS
FOR HANS VOGT

1
Walking, stopping in
Mid-stride

Leaning on air, word on the tip
Of the tongue

2
In the creases of her finger pointing up
To stress not that, but this, what

Else but

Eloquent minuscule
Horizons of grime

3

Watch the velvet
Black
Big
Birdspider piano
Finger his moonlight
Sonata, eight arpeggios
To cross
Your bed

4

All the limbs
But not a stitch

Stretched, then, in their folding, that
Much the more naked

5

Level head, one hundred such,
Hardly to be seen, tilted

Imperceptibly forward, and
If cocked

Not predatory, never a
Mountain top mistily

Bloodying the dreams in it,
Might, no, not even

These might have rectified
The nasty bent

Our species took, ignorant
From desire, gungho with dread

Slow wings beating take
Motion from unharmed air

Around children who break at sunrise
Bread and will not grow old

    Possum breath
— whiff of the One
      Tongue?
        Imagination —

Heard a mouth
      open
        Looked for unicorn (cornered
mirrors) by

Flashlight a ratlike
      baldish creature
Weaving

      Through fresh bark mulch
Pellets, in distant
      Indigo, still driven

To pick among the
      Crusty spitball
        Subterrene (*Nastürmchen!*)
Nasturtium seeds

8

Frowned —

So droopingly
The roof

Tiles overhead
— heavy

Red beef

9

Hellbent, thunderstruck
Piss-asses, locust men
Grope for popcorn, nip the beercan

Gape at a screen

Face cooked
In a helmet
Stole the show for one

10

Head thrown back
Feet skimming the ground, who

Is this coming so fast she's
Lost from sight?

11

Scorched wizard
Sloped indoors, heard his babies

— A Squelch of organs — uncorked
A bottle of Ghost,

Ate his Lantern, slept, in his high
Horse head, catastrophic, nought

But song of a katydid:
Darkening a mountain, shaking out

The hair of the world

12

God, pining for whom helps
Keep some slim

Strip from this, pray, tormented
Skeleton the wobbling

Fat rolls that make him speak
Instead of thunder, with a squeak

13

Heavy logistical weapons of muscle mass rush
Up front to fling
A stone

Hated squirrel
Gulps another mouth-
Ful of bird-

Seed frisks

High / lightly   His tail
Melts into the trees

14

Not the eyebrow, its
Traject, not the gorgon

Hairmass, lady,
What is it, this

Mirrorless me
Topples them

Cracking, somehow
Into your pit?

15

Cuff tucked
Back, palms up to

Help you squinny at
Her cuts

16

A gartered swinger in the human tree
Enjoys her husbands to the tune of three

Her flesh still willing when they hit the floor
She signals for a half half dozen more

Those being spent, her art not stopped, she
    swings
Up, to catch her breath, her heart on other things.

17

Glossy, not from clinging, these
Knuckles predecease her quilt —

Eyelid sliding back peels a white,
Now she called a name, joyfully, it was mine

But in the country she came from
Girls divined their fortunes

In shapes of wax they sprinkled hot,
At random, over water

18

Dry smell, dark yellow
    tugs at heart thongs —
old leatherbound books, bays glow,
    drifting,
when first light stirs up
    the pure fume

With cabbage
Leaf ears
Pinned back and young
Stumbling elephant steps I ran
Up to you,
Poetry, but almost
You had forgotten

Me, you
Gave me a lick,
Delicate and
Suspicious, the way
A lion, lowering
His tongue,
Drinks

    Hollering into the
   Pool
A wild
  Peony of boys
    Lobs its petals

As limestone through smoke
    goes amber
      so goes the world

Through my slit eyes, clenched
    hands, when I
      write these poems

4

A Pinwheel

In his luggage X had stowed a green
Bronze arrowhead. The thing
Came from Armenia, Persian, he said.
Successive satraps in its time
Had all the best Armenian horses herded
South to the Persian king,
Rugs, tubs of turpentine, oil in jars,
Boys tactfully picked —

On the mantelpiece
Y had a stemmed
Wooden cup from Crete. A convict
Made it. You might think
Fingernails not a knife had oddly
Whittled its
Maze of facets, groping for the tilt
It had to stand at. Piss gold the colour
That man's privation wept
And sorrow sweated into it —

Since 1940, Z
Has kept a coin, Macedonian. Curly head
Of Zeus on one side. Philip II
Leans forward, if you turn it, on a high
Stepping horse. Silver tunic still

Flutters around his body,
Silver hat brim twisting in the wind —
Years to go before the drink got him
Or bugles blew, at crack of dawn, and Alexander
Floated off, unblinking, in a cloud of archers.

A Different Banquo

FOR ALBERTO DE LACERDA

A ghost speech
I bring you, with my voice.
When you have gone, my voice will be forgotten.

Ghost speech I
Said, friends. But it's not quite
So far along. Here we are, if still we are

Not yet dead,
Nor gaga. True, any
Moment, any, could for ever extinguish,

Think of it,
The wave. So I ask you:
Remember things I said for fun, not insult,

Even when
Your ears, I said — they're big,
Can you wag them? Or: your lisp kissed sawdust. That

Little mole
On the tip of your nose —
A beacon? Could it guide through storm a long ship?

Can you switch
It off? Does it send up
Punctual signals? Intrusive things like that

I said. In
Hope you'd be provoked. In
Fear a soul might then respond, giving me back

Tenfold the
Joy it was to be there,
Humbly, with you, facing you, in natural

Light. The crust
Of this planet under
Us. Or yawning through our reckless candle flames

The abyss,
Unaccountable. To
Your memory admit me and my weird jokes;

The help I
Ever was to you need
Be no further concern. Still, hold against me

Failings, or
Possibly pettiness
I showed at times when talk ran wild, was too grand

— When you die,
I said, Lord, you'll say, back
I come now, but he'd never known you were gone —

For a voice
Can be wrenching, can pluck
Out of a sky the moon, full, mute, properly

Blent with it.
Yet will you raise me up
Again, at your feasts? Also in lonely rooms

Which exist?
Drink whole flasks of me, raw
Red wine, never negligent? Give me a chance.

As for what
I wrote — thumb through it on
Weekdays, and skip, if you will, the rotten bits.

Or else, by
And large, have done with it.
Save your breath to resist contenders, who kill;

Cruel pack
Rats, they are organized
And horror has no end. Acquiescent, I

Cried out, but
The sound in that cry was
Gashed by evil's claw. Heart now full, vacant soon,

At the beck
And call, leastways, of drab
Manipulators, don't we all bide our time?

Little mouse,
With your voice now I shriek,
So small I made myself, hoping to slip through

Power's mesh.
Not good enough. I had
Chosen to be trapped. To be free was far too much

Breath wasted.
So greed abolishes
Good things, and the canny have no place to go:

Thus we loved,
We did, wildly, trusting
One passion. For, divisible, we only

Loved one voice
Soaring, not mine. It comes
From the sky, weeps, laughs, shakes into shape our trees.

Richard Lion Heart

His country, what a place to have lived in:
Farm girls bringing milk for free, taste of berries,
Sunshine all summer long, the salmon leaping,
Snow crisp in winter, smoke from cottage fires.

I'll ride beside my king on horseback,
Rock hard river valleys hear him sing:
His new song in langue d'Oc for the redbreasts
Goes to the tune of silver horsetails flicking.

In time a wise anarchy will be possible.
Bursts of laughter have washed away oppression,
If anyone wants to govern, gracious people do.
He'll cure my wart and I will clean his crown.

No whining nasal voices, no la-di-da,
No craving for empire, no rotting industries;
Village ponds and words and coastlines are unscummed,
No scummy timid souls could haunt that England.

In Byzantium we'll booze it up, feast with friends
In the south of France. Ah, didn't they clap him
Into a dungeon? I'll spring him. Past far timberlines
We'll clatter on mules and ask the way to Japan.

Lento

To be almost unable to wake up
To see the shadow of a spider's web
To be interested in it sleepily

To notice that the shadow is active
To wonder about its reiterated movement
To think its movement varies from time to time

To call it ocean
To feel it living in the room
To lie full length in the golden light the room contains

To hear the clatter of plates in the courtyard
To forget the shadow of the spider's web
To open the door and approach the plates

To feel hunger
To recognize that your hunger is privileged
To raise your arms

To take a knife in one hand
To take in the other hand a fork
To consider the veins in the marble table top

To admire on your plate a grilled ocean
To eat a helping of spider pie
To taste the white infinitive wine

Tadpoles in the Toulourenc

The frog factory is made of brilliant water,
Pools of it propel the great croak on
And weather willing frill
The Ventoux ramps, come August.

Water: but what bubbles from the ground
Higher up and trims the mountain so,
Exactly where its time begins and what
Comes out of it, has to be chance.

What has to be frog? Some visible pulse
Hangs on; down current or up, across,
Commonly with an incipient
Tip of itself. Numbers, anyhow freakish,

Came up luckier less than often. Tough,
Tough as it was, now perfect valves
Swivel your eyes; critical,
They scour the rocky ground, and see:

Up torrent and down, the not
Unpenetrating Magdalenians, footloose,
Knee deep, chest high in what they drank,
Fingering fire, a bone harpoon point,

At home in it. So too these softer types
Take heart from the rondure of
What they cling to. The frog factory
Is made of brilliant water

And they fancy the fact, never once
Doubting it. No itch, no fuss
To follow the pulse up, through
To the holiness of being frog.

First, silence, then the croak. Us eventual
Bonier harmonies hurt. Roofs of reed,

Starlit canopies of thought we spread;
Domes, electric shields, congested masks

Flicker with appetites our fathomless
Inanity compels. But human voices
Vagabond in the creature chorus can't
Hang on, like these blobs do,

To what they've got. Night, for nobody,
Still it blooms.
    Water, talkative today,
Still their Elephant pumps it out,

Amply. Their Elephant, who, seeing
He knows best, goes most ignored. They
Hang so, by nothing at all
But their own weight.

The Mol

There is a mol and in a lake
She said he lives
And how he sleeps
How deep the water is
How cold and dark

Boatmen shiver and the mol
Lifts his mouth like this
She imitated it
Her jaw flew out an inch
She snapped at nothing

There he is and once a rope
Weighted with a stone
They lowered it for miles
Something tugged at it
They pulled it up she said

The rope was bitten off
The stone had gone
They tried a chain
The chain went down and down
The chain was bitten off

She said he doesn't hurt
He only wants to sleep
The mol is gentle yes
He goes like this
A mouth (I thought) we feed

Halicarnassian Ghost Dialogue

What can the old fool have been looking for?
Back there we had the Many in the One.
If he looked back, this is what he saw:
A ridge, a contour, stark, like an eyelid,
Framing a shrub or two. Barefoot
A little girl, where the lane lofts its dust,
Dragging branches back to a hovel.

He never saw her. If he heard
The heaven bird warble in the pines
And the wind foreveraftering, still
On he went,
Not anxious that his donkey might break down,
There'd always be another; but he hugged
A secret such a fool knows nothing of.

As in a dream a man's thought swings
Many ways between his times, touching
Past and present, hangs between
Dithering signs that sparkle in the vault
Of his flesh, and others, buoyant, yet
More dim, pained, and these
Exact a meaning from him, they propose
To be restored, whole, put back beyond
His death, their origin, the one thing
He never will have known — so he swung
Out, and capably

The donkey trotted under him, unaware
Of all the torchlit cities, fumes, of horns,
Remote, and ceremonies, deaf to voices
That reeked or howled or sang
Sayso into his cranium.

It was the story
Of a girl with a branch, you might say;
Of a hill, stark, contour
Framing sage and oleander. How come,

Everything was changed? He alone
Could sit in the cool and figure, not afraid,
Pen in hand, the monstrous variables,
Plotting their tracks.

         The air, this
Excited us all. None but a few
Did anything about it. A rose, a white
Pebble, look good; at nightfall, in the mouth
A taste of olive. Nothing was enough
To make much palaver about. Wounds, quivering,
Suck the world into their vacuum, when —
When curiosity like his whets its hook
On the air between impulse and action.

There was no story till he tugged
The atoms together.
         Not only for his own good
Does a man pan from dust a glint
Of original information. Spinnakers

Of oddity, majestic
The ripple of ideas, these, our thread,
Irreducible amalgam of our discourse,
He combed from the gabble of old salts,
Horsemen, crones, bandits.

         Listen, was it
His feeling that any heap
Of rags, palpitating on a roadside,
By a tethered goat, or roping hay
Into a sack, has something to speak of;
That any individual is ringed
By a glowing exoskeleton, the tissue
Of stories and of dreams it craves to tell?

And his eye magnified it into a folly of wands,
Ligatures, with pennons cracking,
Cones, strained pulleys, psyche
Thinging itself into an essential

Funniness, a pupa, something
Like birdsong, or
A ship of resistance, and of wonder
An instrument. No one girl
Who drags her branch down a lane
Matches any other.

This exciting air, this
Time, this phenomenal
Melting skin,
        chrysalis of inventions, thickened

With sorrow, so he imagined it,
With such zest — no choice, but to display,
He forced it to, colour, with strangeness.
He loved it so, stripped
Or like a woman who walks, walks
As a tree might, or a fountain at daybreak,
Unfathomable.

Was he saying that home, after all,
Depends on the difference you make of it;
Wild, like a sheen; in a heron's eye,
Pigment? Any domain
Warms to delight, hopelessly fragile,
When someone sets a rose,
Fresh, in the middle of a dinner table.

No. He was saying that this little girl
Was born alone, lived alone, dies alone.

Ayasofya

The long bird trails his feet,
Flying over water.
    Not a perch hereabouts
He does not know; but a dome
Mirrored in the water sprays its topaz
    Treasures up, and moans
Beneath his flight's
    Bowstroke.

And another flits into the dome
Through the star of a broken window,
Quicker, the dove;
    A shelf, tilted,
Tops a column, from a stick
    Nest a cry, shrill,
Has magnified its volume, striking
Under the roof angle a mosaic
    Alexander.

Dome, hive, unspeakable the mass,
Honey of power, down
    Age after age it slid
Into and out of you. Still she squats,
Bent, in the black gutter,
    Sightless, turning
Now and again to the sun her flat
    Scabbed face.

An Old Wine Press

An old wine press
With its iron screw
Column down the middle —
Vertical slats doubly hooped
Contain the tub — this instrument
Sepia on account of its being
Not the very thing but a photo dated
No later than 1910

Higher up, steep slant of a barn roof.
The line of its eave like a lip,
Wavy. A sort of monster
Grin goofily reveals
The stubs of seven teeth, unless
These are beam ends or swallows' nests

And halfway up the slant
Two holes are built, like little eyes, or else
They breathe for the hayloft, handy
Homes of dove, dark lodges
For the grape scented air

All this no more than a glimpse
But the barn behind the wine press caught
And carries onward
A human imprint, rough hewn
A flicker of the torch

Here for once
Doubly precious, considering these
Eight people grouped around the press:

Just a bunch of farm folk, three generations,
The men clothed in stained denims, sweaty caps;

The woman has pinned a flower to her breast
And holds an empty cheese basket;
A little boy had curled his fingers
Around the handle of a hooped
Wooden wine jug

There they stood, tilting
Every which way; splay feet, beefy arms
Dovetailed into a right good
Angular design:

    Three men
Lean against the tub on its platform;
If this beard might crumple into a king's mask,
Still clog and boot crack with mud
And glue these
Dancers to the ground; the boy
Hangs in the middle, perched, dangling
Tiny booted feet —

Any moment
The glass he grips by the stem will spill;
Oddly tender yet, the way
All around him thicker fingers hold
The scarce seen cool substance —
In it gleams the god, red and savage,
Spinning the world for more than money

Yet the money matters. You can plot
Grim pursuit of it in the skew
Cheek folds of the white-haired man.
Hope made the woman's mouth
A thin long line and in her round chin
Totted up
Credits of hair, winnings of eye, decimals
Of nostril

Who knows, it is mostly too late;
The wine that time at least
Had a fair chance;
The footwear might see another ten years out,
As good as a second skin, these denims
Are worn as the sun
Wears its light, or as the god they nourish
Squid-wickedly has thrown
History over his tentacles, a robe
Smoky in colour, a tissue of bloodstains,
Whose, fading, sepia

Mezzomephistophelean Scholion

The place of his birth: some few conjecture
It was Athens. After all, in a letter,
He laid claim to the title 'Attikos'. Others
Find reason to suppose that he was born
In Nicomedia. The chronicle, they say,
Written by Michael Attaliatos might be construed
To identify Michael Psellos with Michael
The Monk of Nicomedia.

    We, on the other hand,
Cannot concede that our Michael (Psellos)
Ever did the sort of thing
The Monk is said to have done.
    Nor can we reconcile
Attaliatos' apologias for Psellos
With his poor opinion of that Monk. More,
Psellos has it in a letter (no suspicion
Of any scribal lapse) that first he saw
The light of day close to the monastery
At Narsos.

    There is no cause to doubt
His testimony, either, that he was sixteen
When Romanus Argyrus died, and twenty five
When Constantine Monomachos granted him
A minor secretarial post.
    The date of his birth
Can accordingly be reckoned without error
By persons not unversed
In the history of the Macedonian Renaissance.

    It will be known to all
Who take pleasure in the learning of that time,
The sinuous paintings, luminous artifacts,
And subtle scriptures.

        In so far as the scroll
Of history reforms behind us
Its convolution, but spells
Persistent shadowy figures across
The curve in it we scratch, or tap, and trample on,

        It will be significant
To such as choose to find in that time
A foothold, and from the glow as on great moonlit peaks
Of its regard for the old thinkers
Draw increase of consciousness, courage from its
Unflinching critique of desolate Asian demonologies,
And in its Hellenizing northward drift
See for pity
Among the Slavic peoples and languages
Fortune stripped naked.

Irish

Here as the bamboo
leaf and rod
glisten
in broken moonlight
this harp music

I suppose it echoes
the strings of rain, silver
those dark pools
drink up
on streets in Ireland

Say time could have taken
a different shape,
but this, with red eyes that weep
and search the horizon
choose we did

Say a spirit got
knotted
in spilt intestines, a body
of music shattering
the bamboo door

Now leaf and rod,
the fawn I saw stopped
in a clearing, pulsars in moth-
eaten velvet
flash slow beacons

But a perception chosen
digs historic
claws deep down, not
like the bamboo rhizomes
they touch dancing

Pickled
in this whiskey bottle was
a heart, do not listen
the wind sings in its
ventricle, seaward

In Memory of Peter Szondi

He is writing the words
smaller and smaller, no drift
betrays the question, every twist of it
a stitch in the garment, a drop scripted
into the river, still smaller
the drops contract,
so far in fact their intervals absorb
not a trick of the heavenly
changes of light, instead
gunshot is packed, proof,
into a cartridge.

   The original
text still resists, crackerjack, but he
drinking the poison of power out of it
tightens his grip and over
the absent mind of his composite
adversary maps
another compound, gray, sees his automatic
quill soon, horrified sees
bursting from his head

     Gunbarrel blue
searchlight beams raking a beech wood —
old words, once floated breath,
buckle under his gist, their stockade
tangled ugly knuckles,
a scalp shaven, these are skeletons, their
scripture reeks of carbolic.

     Something else
has him by the throat,
something else calling the shots, his
discipline a terror, his protective
passion sapped by the microbe,
intolerable ache
of millions driven living

into the gas, he checks
the clock, walks out unbent
by the weight of his coat, he thinks
the river is that way, full stride
he walks
at last powerless into it.

Cabaret de la Canne, January 1855

Sir, I do not know your name,
Nor do you know mine. So we sit,
Briefly, at neighbouring tables, you
With your bottle, the cat on your knee,
I with my little glass.

In our sunken ship
The third table has been taken
By the fine man of darkness, whom
We do not see. Look, on the furrowed surface
Glittering still, the flake of snow I flicked
From the collar of my coat when I came in.

Each sits watching
The face of his own slowly turning
Universe. Particularly the cat
Has known how the heat
Comes and goes. Important smells
Wrinkle and flex into signatures, you know,
Writ small in snowflakes and the skeletons
Of leaves. Shuddering,
The fingers of a spirit ink into our skins
Mysterious names, numbers, and messages.

Ancient gutters
Accommodate the cat, providing
Fish, spare ribs, a scrap of lamplight;
Spilt milk to lap up, now and then.

There are places where people turn yellow,
Having nothing to eat. Cloacas, attics.
Broken roofs. Through holes the snow sifts.
A Valois song can be issuing, in another street,
From a little girl's lips
For a penny.

Mandolins, a lantern swaying, make it
Difficult to want less than a tree to dance with.

Do we suffer
Most because the bunched worms will hang
In the emptiness you are looking at, this
Dome of mine, bald, this bony cabin?
    What is immortal
If not the injustice?

There was a room I lived in once,
I remember how the early light in it
Fell across two rescued Fragonards.
There was a girl, nearly naked she was,
Tigers ran before her on a leash
And a little donkey woke us, braying,
Or a barge trumpet's echo off the river.

Like a swift in his globe of crisp mud
I hung between sleep and waking
And heard the straw speak in my thin
Mattress. Look, here it is, another face
Of that same
Towering light, again
In this bit of a rainbow, at its peril
Afloat in the eau-de-vie:
I drink it for the dream that spills
Into life.

They tore it down, it was an old house.
They did not tear down
The other room, which, if you follow me,
We put there, suspending it
Outside any space that iron balls
Can shatter.

In that room the last vine still grew,
A veiny green, very ancient.
The last vine, first planted when
The emperor was Julian and Paris Egypt.
From the vine,
Yes from it you might see
A light as from the original stars unfolded

And flew as it pleased, to vary
As it touched the featured walls through
Twelve emotions. With snaky lines
It marbled the stones and old chairs
We had broken by leaning back to laugh.
To eye the stones was to feel a flow
Of female warmths and hear the goddess, —
Moan and shriek of the sistron in her fingers.

What can you be thinking?
No, do not indispose the cat.

The Bow

A little arrangement
The table neat
Napkins folded

An arrangement
Any casual act forefelt
Hums with a thought's movement

A plan to get up in the night
For a wild
Bit of dancing

Crazy
Planned the
Unpredictable grace

A cuckoo
Moment we
Plan it and die of it

Two-ply such
A delicate
Tendon

Tautens
You great
Bow of civilization

Conundrum on a Covenant

When did we mean to meet? I never saw you.
Each time I came, you'd gone. Now at my door
You rap, and I'm not there. Write me letters:
Your scrawl divined, how should I open them?

Forest and other calendars you flew through,
Tasting of alcohol, armpit, lotus —
I'm not there. You stand me up, thanks, but
Which of us broke the date, will break the word?

Etymology: it says there has to be, occult
In the abiding nature, before your finer breath
Fathoms the bowl of this bent lily pond,
A place for the likes of us to palaver in.

Or lifting a glass you might have shown,
Surfaced, in a bar. My eyeballs, had they,
Ghastly, swivelling, tipped the whole pipkin,
Brimful as a sundial, upside down?

Ah yes, I saw, smelled, heard. The rosy
Gloss of a thumbnail. Musk, a key change
Spread you. In her believed *feels* and *explores*,
Orphaned Opal d'Orléans, you blessed her.

Muck, too, in a blot of muck I hear, some days,
Mute, goofball, your unstemmed galaxies
Croaking. But where in the world are we to converge on?
Suspense electric — nerves that hummed snap,

Less than a smatter, plot wilts, large characters
Fidget in the wings . . . Who can pretend
Now to picture you? Snarled up, acid,
This air I breathe holds not a trace of you.

Cherries

Cherries, cherries on their cherry trees
Across a snowy slope of architecture
Is this what he has to say and all of it
The pilot with a responsible face
Eyes that grip and penetrate everything

But now the world has come to an end
A squall from the southeast levels
The last buildings
My mother young and candlelit dithers in the church
My father never dead at all runs to the door
Anxious, waving a hand to her

Besides, in albums there are clay replicas of Roman coins
Shelved in this shop with old enigma books
Funny it is stuck in an airport
Besides, I have eaten the inside of a bread pie
And now this stickleback still twitching
I gobble it up and wonder at my greed

The world has come to an end
So what is to be said about the cherry trees
The snowy slope
I am climbing the stairs to where I spoke to my toys
Three top rooms are filled with beds
Double doors close over one bed of cherry wood
Fitting the headboard I make it into a tombstone
So what about sheets

And walking behind me in her nakedness
This girl has no place
This girl
Only eighteen tonight she has no place to sleep
A spit curl cannot hide the end of the world
The worry in her face her unknown face

Doussa res we are looking for the warmth I suppose
Should we take the bed with doors

Jump in just as we are and shut the doors on ourselves
But I am stooped like a barometer
A giraffe in this immeasurable Africa my flesh
Has chewed up every sprig of love that ever was in me

The Few Objects

The few objects on a table
Do not read the papers
No sweat breaks out on them
When they work their gentle bells
To tinkle for a pilgrim
They do not startle, nervous
When he lifts a hand
In doubt, in apprehension

Rosenkavalier Express

Sundown in the dining car of the Rosenkavalier Express —
    I am seeing the packed trees and fields of wheat,
Dense greens involved with depths of indigo,
    For the sun — all day it shone like nobody's business,
And I think that a poem should be like these
    Packed trees and wheat, a tuft aglow, an indigo thing;
Then for a split instant I'm happy, a thrill goes through me,
    The dinner of beef and wine, shock of a salty
Taste in the beef, the red ordinary wine,
    Might account for it, but robuster than any reason,
Visceral or not, is the briskness of it, I mean
    The spasm, spliced with a sweet twinge of doubt
Whether I'd ever be up to voicing a poem like that.

And there was the whole day sunlit in Vienna,
Hungover a bit after hours of drink with friends;
    I am still out on a walk at one in the morning,
The big idea was to find, at last, the Mikado,
    But I couldn't, so now I'll never be sure
If a special whore called Josephine hangs out there.
    I am still strolling around at one in the morning
Though it is eight p.m. and as the train swings
    Westward into the night, fields will be warm as beds,
A peace envelops me from eyebrow to anklebone,
    I want to say thank you to someone for letting me
Eat and drink and feel on my flesh, whizzing by,
    These tufts of pine, these depths of indigo,
Rhombs of wheat that surge in the wind;
    Birds and rabbits will be rustling through them,
Smells drift, sprung by sun from June rain,
    Prickly smells of wing and fur, rose and lettuce,
Search in me for the tautest bowstring, holding
    But lightly holding the midpoint of the bow.

Ah well, the Mikado stroll was a washout,
    But with coffee there comes a little sugar packet
With "Mikado" printed on it, and a gasp, childish

Enough — I catch my breath as the large
Rhythm of coincidence wraps me in a fold of fire.

What is this? Moneyless but sometimes lucky
I have been ways with women that made them powderkegs.
Wrong, time and again, I have wounded people,
Fallen short of their dreams, risen to them
Too little or too late; less and less I can tell
What feeling is good for, but have been acquainted
With animals fierce and beautiful, so to whom,
To what should I give thanks, and thanks for what?

What have I brought to love, if not catastrophe?
Now ideas flock like moonsheep in my turning head,
Now I see roof angles, wooden cabins in cabbage plots,
Goalposts and staircases, and so rotund a hill,
O, distance slips into its blue mist, but point blank
Stalks of wheat and blades of grass freshen again.
As if through me Imagination wanted, sightless,
To fondle the volumes of objects and read their legends,
Trim old barns and now the Danube, full stretch,
Open lips that motion to speak, wag their tongues.

So I think of the tongue of a blackbird,
And that I won't call this moody aria "Mitteleuropa."
Grateful not to be dead, or frightened, or oppressed,
I think of the call in the song of a blackbird:
When you patrol the dust of Mitteleuropa
It doesn't perceive that you and history are there;
It sings with a voice that must be dreaming
It is a petal and so, rosily, all for free,
In one cool fold of fire the petal wraps you.

Apocrypha Texana

1

Gravity with Popcorn

First comes
The popcorn tree

It is very still
To be seen with blue

Behind it hoping
Gravity so

Simply intended
Marking the time

Construction workers
Dream of popcorn

Most but less
Of mud festoons

And rabbits listening
Less for the clang

Of snow perhaps
Hear the popcorn

Whistling now
To keep me warm

I stretch my plums out
Still somehow

And never no more
Need movie-going

Local Roads

These local roads they say
In Texas hug their curves
Or cracks and hollows
Like ancient pain

I looked ahead
I thought a turtle or what else
A flexing clump a shell
Had waddled half across

I ran to find if I was wrong
But there it was
Again the vacant womb
A god imagined human music from

My impulse the reverse
I slipped that hood back on
I shrank into the shell
To shield a scaly head

Whirled into the air I heard
Colossal whistling shoes
And fingers beating time
But vaguely on my back

Caught up with me at last
What century was this
My negligible weight
How balanced in his hand

Scars of ancient lightning
Scollop the vaulted shell
What if they broke open
What frenzy would he feel

Driving Home

Imagine you might forget
The white road
Splitting away from the black road

Not loaded words

Imagine you
Might forget its whiteness and
In the identical moonlight

A different smell of burnt cedar

But it was never white was it
A gray blue gone to violet rumpled
Like denims in a surplus store
White road — pulverized

Limestone bathed in the rays

You might forget the fork imagine
Sound of the owl further down the road
Splitting your time
Between now and the hearing of it

A voice inappositely pink
O whiskered shrimpish owl

But then you never forgot
Pursuing the tubes of light
How it felt

More like a branching tree than a church
Made ghostlier
By the fact of a candle in it

Never so new
It was not to be afraid

Imagine
Talking and happy stripped
Inside not even shutting the door
The forgotten embrace

Now when you came together
It will nourish
All the ways everything moves

A Portrait of J.L.M.

We called him spirit of the place,
But he's more like a good old tree root.
Went off, a year gone, back to Rockport.
It seems, when he'd gone, us not even
Knowing it, everything fell apart.

    Wish I remembered
What he told me. This bit of town I landed in,
These railroad tracks he'd known, secret
Signs chalked on the freight wagon doors,
Hobos bivouacking, and how he'd drift across,
Talk with them. That was far back
In the Thirties, near enough to the yard on Seventh
He got our big old bamboo from, planted it.

    Wanderings, the split rail
Fences he built, him wiry then as now, bird faced,
Out west of Sanantone; any job he could find
He put both hands to. He belonged with
Boilers of big ships, blue clouds
Of working people on the move, tumbleweed;
You do the most you can.

    Far out hereabouts
He'd gone courting, before big money
Rolled the roads in. Remember now,
Hummed the tune once, he did. They walked out
Through live oaks together, rocks, and cedar,
Listening to the trickle of the creek in Spring.
He sat his Mildred down, kissed her,
Same old tune in their heads.

    I ate her cakes
She'd later bring at Christmas down the hill,
Stopping to chat a while, propped against
The doorpost, she'd laugh like anything
But sometimes she took ill.

Drains, spigots, carburettors,
The pump, I saw his knuckles whiten
When he fixed them, and later his hand
Shook, breath caught, and as he worked
His mouth helped, with twists and lippings.

Rolled his own cigarettes; told me —
Here's this old song book, found it at the county dump,
You want it? 1865 — Irish songs. Irish
As his Indian scout grandfather had been. He'd
Told him of hilltops hereabouts

Where the Indians hunkered,
Yawning. And how a coach might rumble by,
Gold or guns in it, stuff they could use. And how
Into this cave his grandfather went once, deep,
Now they've blocked it, but it goes underground
All the way from the lake to Tarrytown.
A volcano, too, he said.

I might not believe it,
Not so far off, east, he found obsidian there,
Beyond where the highrise banks and turnpikes
And the military airport are. Trees,
He loved trees and drove miles to see them
At their best, the right time of the year.
Buckeye and catalpa in their first flower,
Chinaberry, dogwood.

All birds had ordinary names,
Like redbird, but once in a while he'd speak
Old words, not from books but from Tennessee,
Like once he said "quietus." Always
Flesh in his words, and bone, and in his doings,
Not absent even from the way he'd knock
A bourbon back, straight, that was the way
He liked it, then roll another cigarette.

For Mildred when her teeth
Fell out he whittled deer horn so she'd have
A biting edge up front. When he came by, dressed
Smart for a visit, he'd be wearing false
Rat teeth up front and give a wicked grin.
There was this park he kept,

He knew all the weeds in it,
All, and told how some weed sent
Cows mad and was taken too much liberty with
By them young folks as went out there
For a high time.

Well, then he'd push off
In his battered pickup, headed for a honkytonk
Some place down the line. Why don't folks look at
That kind of man? Some say insight
Comes when you tell the individual
Get lost. What's all their deep droning talk
To him? He's too smart to think up
Revolutions, what's it, that perspective stuff?
Maybe he's nobody

But he made things work,
Never slaving, nor ginrollizing. Made things
Shift and level with every breath he drew.
Had no grievance, spoke no ill of anyone
Or anything save spindly offshoots
Of tree roots that split drainpipes in the country,
Having ballooned in them, like brains
Got swole, so he'd say, with all the excrement.

Visio Reginae Coeli

A hunchback pulls the last python out of a tank.
Bony women crouch around a pail.
Slithering from the sky these roasted crows
Print their silhouettes on a rock wall.

Not yet: safety in numbers. Casually bricks
Replace forest; valves, windows are fitted.
Not passion but neglect postpones a touch
That finally could lift the roof off.

Induplicable a breath
Lets a lady call to her gardener.
Morning glistens in the fragonard sprays.
Elm roots draw a deep earth liquid up.

Still in rooms the spoons clink against glass,
Objects rustle, delicately moved; the fanged
And happy twiddle their thumbs, now heaven's queen
Swoops across the sky, descending in her robe,

A blue, a crimson. Closer now, unbidden,
Through the ring begun by her motion,
Fathomless music winged with voices
Lifts all her creatures into the air.

Pinyon Incense

Oblong a pellet
In a small
Pueblo bowl

Careful
It could come to bits
A fleck like conscience

Burn as you light
One tip
And breathe on it a pang

Possibly a finger
Writing but
A fresh piece

And firm shoots mysterious blue
Scented smoke up
If ever the smoke thins

Look while ash
Blackens the tip it is
Not standing on

Down through the spirals move
Meet
Old man trombone brown

He stands
Where his feet keep him
At a cave opening

Watch the writ of furrows
Groove his dry
Pine bark

Palm he is
Not angry now he simply will not
Let you in

With your sorrow
And your bodyful of pacts
Broken

Let him say
Sorrow let him say
Nothing

Just cup like that his
Palm and cuff
The top of your head off

A Lyric to Stanley Myers's "Cavatina"

(In John Williams' guitar arrangement)

Blue cave, deep stream,
Stream, how you run;
Flow, clear, from the blue cave
For the sun to shine on.

Old sun, clear stream,
Not made for the pain;
Still you receive us,
Now and again.

High, high the falcon calls,
Mocks the world as he flies;
His shadow dips across the stream,
Silver, in the sunrise . . .

What means is not the end
But the movement of such things;
Watch the falcon move to the beat
And yielding of his wings.

Now there is this place, love,
Where we could belong —
A wave means to carry us
In the secret of a song.

Enough, enough that we flow
As often as we fly —
Not counting, old stream,
Time gone by.

A Young Horse

Where can it now have gone
The warm night ruffled
With screech owl feathers
Where can it have gone
When the horse came to a call

The warm night with branches
Haunt of moss web of intelligence
The breath of a young horse
Cooling between fingers
The night vast with bunched stars

Simply blown away it was
The night murderous and milky
The night of old hymns and hot bullets
Blown away by a breath
Curling between fingers

It flew between my ribs
It set a hollow throbbing
Between the ribs and fingers
A sort of pulse had shuttled
Felt as it wove and melting

Melting the shell this mortal
Man nocturnally hides in
His temple void of presence
With a wicket gate of muscle
To shield from shock his hungers

People in Kansas, 1910

1

Now they stand quite still on level doorsteps,
Outside the Drug Store and the Post Office.

A white sky, two buildings underneath it,
Outside the buildings half a dozen people.

Across the dust like dice the buildings rolled,
Stopped under the white sky.

Soon the people prised them open, clambered out.
Here at last. Here, they said, is Dorrance.

2

Stiff, like effigies, almost,
Made of language; speaking
The people came to be real for one another.

A head below the P of the Post Office
Shrinks into a Stetson. A wiry woman
Shoulders the stone Drug Store doorpost.

All six like effigies, wax, mechanical.
Work all day with corn, beans, soda pop.
The letters, few and far between. Senseless.

3

The people insist. But a vague terrain —
How can you fill it. Corn and letters
Stop short. The horizon,

A banker might one day darken it,
Locomotives. This big space frightens. We
Lost here a sense of belonging with the wind,

Now geese and trees that fly with it are no part of us.
Trust your shirt, these oblong blocks of stone.
Trust two dark heaps dropped in the dust by horses.

A chimney pot, back of the Post Office. Plain
Undistressed people, you never dreamed
Of burning letters, one by one, or bodies.

4

That's it. None could know what later crooked
Shapes
History takes when something radiant
All the brain and body cells cry out for
Is suppressed

Behind bars appetites riot; captured
Guards
Sob for mercy; spies are fucked.
These oblong people lived out their free time
On credit,

They could count it wise not to wish
Their soap
Were sweeter, small business not
So methodical, dogs happy to work
Nights for them.

No. Their stark speech I do not understand.
Why
Make of life such a hard nut?
Or did they? Far off, faceless, kin of mine,
Hard living

Salt of the earth, sharply defined, crystal
Flakes,
You were never as oblong
As the buildings that warmed and warped you.
You weren't fooled.

5

Focus again,
So sharp you can smell the cigar,
The string beans taste

Just right. Objects, it
Was not your fault, objects, if
That is what you were, you have to go

Forth, shoulder your signs
In capital letters, onward to a place
I tell you of,
A place of blue and yellow. There
Mountains and people are one indivisible creature,
A grape admits night glow
To become its body,

Absolute, good as the bread
Is dense to the teeth
With death and legend. There, with patience
And the scent of sage,
People other than you ripened once
To a style — some to foreknow
And resist evil. Goodbye

Innocent oblongs, forget nothing
Now it is too late, but
Forget my fist with which if I could
I'd bang this postage stamp through
Into the reversed
World you stand in. It

Would stick in your sky of whiteness,
Perforated, a script of waves,
Muttering to you,
A voice, cancelled:
The sun does not shine for anyone,
The leaf arrives one breath
Only before the wind.

The Mason

came up from Patzcuaro, he said
where the women sell white lake fish,
seventeen women and seventeen fish
all wrapped alike, fish and women, how to choose,
how, in that old market, I ask you,
the right identical
fish

But he came with a chisel
two pieces of wood, one string,
four months flat he worked over these stones,
limestone arches, lintels, coping stones for a well,
hot here, he'd say, not like my
mountains, and he dressed the stone
in a fashion

Nobody hereabouts even wanted to know,
like this, with his chisel and string,
him going on seventy, look
the grooved small diagonals, curved
like fruit, colour of bone the
shouldering, floated into position every face
by touch, he wouldn't so much as
wink at a power tool

One night coming home the house
in total darkness
Could he be there with his homebound Indio
assistant, they'd be
talking Tarascan, found them both
sitting in the dark (that wooden room) and calm,
folded hands, being silent

And of an elevator he said one day
in a city building: Funny,
into that little room you go and other folks wait
outside while you wait inside a bit until
the door slides back open, folks
are still outside, but how come
they're different?

Lines

Never thought but once to walk there, solo;
How the places change — the rage, the spin.
When a death call comes with the sun —
Feel her hair echo soft in your fine hands,
And sweep severally the leaves from the door.

Thermodynamics

Moving in a blanket
About the house,
A blue blanket enveloping most of me
This first cold November night, I meant to ask,
Warming to the blanket,

Just what is the time now,
What century am I living in,
Am I a monk, this hovering floor, tiles,
If I kneel, hard on the bones
Of anyone hit by spirit,

Would it hold, besides,
A moment still, another time silkily
Respond to me? Rich
In the rising wind brocades — am I a samurai? —
Billow, fish head hat gone slap

Through the roof
Hoists me into the sky almost,
Squids, ho-hum,
Vaguely bob, odd, below my junk navy, half
The way to China, medieval weather

Supervenes and soon
Vast carpets of sand coalescing
Fashion the glass
Two fingers and a thumb tilt,
And red Verdillac cools my tongue

Abrupt cut — how come
A blue poilu I'm cloaked in thunder,
Shellshocked, the mud
Is red, but very deep and smelly,
At Verdun

I lost my grip. Higher than cloud
South today, navigating by

The continental backbone,
A V of geese flew on
And on: blanket of sounds, vagabond,

Be damned, honk of geese, a crack
When the timber two-by-fours
Cool or a beam
Contracts — even the wine has hit the spot,
Finding a little sanctuary

To be astounded at, but nevermore the real
Paroles reveal a volume, rasping
After all, distinct
As once a weathervane, old,
Spun a void, or words

Dovetailing, veiled it, in the bowl
A seventh, uneventful peach
Spirits the symmetry
Back, a globe still
Hangs in air over a lake with swans

Minim

White owl over
Surface of a stream
No idea
What supports him

A Road that is One in Many

FOR GEORGE AND MARY OPPEN

This is a little road, this part of it
Like the centre bar of an old hand drill
Runs straight from this bend to the next

Hold tight when you walk along it
Violet orbs revolve under the pebbles,
Daily shadows. These vines have grapes

Shrub vines, bitter grapes, mustang. Hold tight
When this bird spider hauls his thick ass
Over the tarmac, this pothole is his

Hold tight to your straight walk, tiptoe
Certain spots are swept by heat
That is what blows, that is what dries

The inside of your mouth. The signs
Droop or rust, are not adequate
To the events they warn about. Warn

The pecan comes late into leaf, the big
Pecan; that is juniper, a cone, house
Of a singing bird. The signs do not sing

Being, but collisions, they take sometimes
A life or two. Hold tight, don't roll off, all
Sorts of people have walked along this road

This road is old, new, was Indian trail
By water, TU, they said, water; now
Corvettes and subarus, few foot people

This field in summer clings to a thatch
Of slow dragonflies; now nothing lives
In the tin shed, or is it nothing, only

Bugs, but you can moo to the ghosts
Of seven extinct preoccupying cows. Not
A slope in sight. These black

Eyed susans are the prettiest flower,
Later the dayflower marks its own distinct
Fluting off against this sky of skies

And the white rain, the white rain lilies
Really are these fragrant acid fruits
Of rain. Soon it stops. Under the polestar

At night hold tight still, grip this
Ground with your unshackled feet,
Don't scare, these vines or ghosts are

Vines and ghosts. At night the lake
Is good for a swim. Don't mind these bats
That flit crisscross close to the cooling

Surface. Hold tight just once again,
Then let go and be consumed by the cool.
This is in the things and shines in the things.

2

Woden Dog

Wot doth woden dog
Por dog drageth plow

Thing odd dog not
Much good plow drager

But por dog drageth
All same plow

More come jellifish
Sting him woden dog

Jellifish in air now
Other odd thing

A speeking maner come
Round back to trooth

So doth dog plow
Plant seed of tree

Por dog life short
Woden dog long hope

Woden dog keep stung
Jellifish all round back

Dog hope tree grow
Much tree grow soon

Dog want find tree
Find releaf releaf

***

Bus drifer pleez
Make a smoth start
If not woden dog fall over

Bus drifer stop graduel
If not woden
Dog hit deck

Pleez bus drifer
Tern corner sofly
Woden dog cant hold on

You no he cant sit
Propper
You no he cant holtite

Forgoet how to life has he
Lest thing nock him sensles
All you no

Woden dog smoth graduel
Woden dog sofly he scare think
You forgoet how to drife

***

Jakit off jus warin sox like mean you
Woden dog reed times ever doggone day
Nites watchin his toob wow
Haffin the noose hapn

Wow fokes I tel you
Woden dog lap up noose

Woden dog bominate seecrit he reely do
Noose noose he bark runnin down street
Galumfin baknforth to his malebocks

He wannit so bad
He wannit to go
Like choclit maltn ketchup
Hole globe pakitchn pree paredn paid fur
Sitn in his noose baskit

No seecrit make woden dog
Bust out in flour one mawnin
Lookit soaps he buy woden dogfood
Killins toon that po looshn stuf
Brung home in his teeth

Come days wen he skratchn say
Mite try killin sumwun to make noose of me
Paps if I make noose of him
He dont done do it?

Woden dog howcom you loss
Yor own seecrit eye sunshine
Woden dog howsit taist that woden dogfood
Whars thet kemel dog
Ever see canser wok a mile
Smokin up a kemel ever see war stop
Juscos you lookin?

Jeez fokes jus thort
If bad stuf stop no mor noose fur woden dog
Wot then ole flee bit dog
You see nuddin to lookat
You jus sit theren cry

***

Whodat
Striden backnforth in orifice
Who *dat*
Givin ordures

Whodat maken long biznis calls
Eatin long biznis bananas
He look horty
My whodat planifikting plitical fouture

Watchout
Here he come zoom by
Zoom silva jet clatter copta
Weekend in Toekyoe?
Meetin Younited Nayshun?

Whodat now
Widda dame in a yot wearin captin hat
Crakin lobsta
My my

Woden dog thats who
Woden dog how smart you done got

***

Hard inside
Woden dog

Woden dog gon
Sniff aroun for mudder

Mudder soft inside
Woden dog dig

Woden dog swetpant
Nuddin come up

No mudder
Dipressed woden dog

Dog shrink gifm pill
How that now help

Dog body keep movin
But inside he nut

No mudder inside
No soft strong mudder

Nuddin in world
Woden dog size

Howls too purty offen
In his dog house dum

So small he feel
Stinkin wikid woden

***

Yes derm dawg
Urmpteen snarls
Make nuddin
No bedder

Yew always countin
Countin crazy dawg
You mean
See me through glass

Derm yew lukn so glum
Like eny doods nuddin
Yew like like yew
Say dancein shit

Call yewsell a dawg
I aint buyin
Yew aint no morna
Cardboard ratlsnaik

Yew mean
Snarlin always makin
Fuss yew bossy think
Me mor stoopidn yew

Maybe too
But I countin
The timesnile git yew
Wunofem

***

Woden dog keep stil
So you can feel it
Movin

Rounanroun whirlin world
Why you keep with it
Is that reel

Woden dog
Keep stil so you
Can feel it movin

***

Hey now
Hoo done got hide
Inside you innerlekshuls

Meckin
Yore gin
Roll I say shuns

Hooz
Moovin yoohoo
All ways tokkin

Wokkin long
Rode like you wuz
Uh ginrollized creekin

Rekkernize hoo
He be my my if it aint are
Ole solom fren dubble you dee

***

Woden dog sittin
On the backstares

Sittin in the dark
Breathin a bit

115

What's this listen
Breathin

Laff
Woden dog

That's it
Laffin on the backstares

Thems wavesnwaves
Them cool backstares

Help dog floatin
Low float high

Not let waves go so
You seem zikazak

Doan it hurt some
Hey woden dog

Not let the laff hole up
In woden dog box

Listen breathin just so
Now no more done hurt

***

Wyso suddn everbody
Rite on walls

FREE WODEN DOG
Anifs time

Like I nevver got
Inclose free

Woden
Dog piksher?

Spose no place else
To rite

***

Silva smoak of pine
Burn chill
Woden dog shivver
Owl not heard

Lightslice fix to floor
Think dead
Woden dog like ice
In his box owl not heard

Owl hoot rainbow
Out of owl eyes
Owl hoot rainbow wonder
Dog not see dog bark at ghost

Owl not heard
Dog munch heap white aple
Not feel snow as owl bountie
Not smell snow rainbow

Woden dog eat heap
Aple up
Pip corn all cold aple meat
Not see owl

Not see some owl eyes
Not hear
How pips look sound yum yum
Crunch owl eyes aple up

Dog wine in boxn stay putn scoff
Woden dog alltime scoff
Woden dog shut in wod
Not smell sweet pine

Woden dog not smell wind song
Burn swingin low
Swingin in pine wod
Owl not hoot fur him in pine log

Owl not hear in dog box
He woden dog
Snow owl hoot that rainbow now
Now hootn touch dog heart

3

After A Noise in the Street

It is the small
Distinct image, old as you like,
On a coin, or silvery
In a daguerreotype

Speaks to me:
The trooper Probus,
Two centimetres high, at most,
Helmeted, sloping

A spear
Across a shoulder,
Condenses all
The gas of empire

Into a few
Quick signs. No fuss, either,
Had perplexed her face,
This young and tawny

Woman, but
An anger, fine, makes
Luminous now the eyes
She levelled in Nebraska

At the lens, never
Exhausting it, for the hands
Folded and slender in her lap
Siphon a torrent

Of feeling through the image.
There is anguish
Untrapped, an ardent
Breath sets free to fall

A dew as on a cherry,
To magnify, by sharpening
So far, the resolute
Infinitesimal flesh, this wisp

Of being, only this
A mortal
Tentatively manifests. A
Measure just

One fraction grander could
Put back
Into the spear
Slaughter;

Distend a pleat
In this dress, or blow
A tassel up
Beyond belief — and it lumbers

Back into the flimflam; an
Embossed cuirass,
Probus any bigger, snagged
In power's mesh

Spills, as a blur, or boast,
His contracted time
Into the heaving
Primordial pettiness.

Hot Bamboo

My roots go
sideways
only
they
will
never
grope deep
nohow can
these
hollow
shafts
hold
remembrance
whenever
sounds
trickle
flute
gong
from
the crackpot's
pretend house
I
want you
moonlight
(if you
will)
to waft
them
over a touch
a merest whiff
will
send
me
responding
with a shiver
on my way
down

again
growing
to the hut
impossibly
a lake
is
there
an early
heron
suspended
in a mist
now
drinks
this
open
sky
limbs
of wild plum hide
old scrolled
mountain
so
spread
your
fan
soon
sighed
bamboo

Jerusalem, Jerusalem

White building under pecan tree
Four poles cradle the porch roof

Beyond gap in branches blue sky trackless
Snoozing in roof slope ghost of a pagoda

White wall veined with leaf shadow
Tree unfolds a boom of spray

Homely air, who knows which way moving
Tree pulse drums, cricket whistles tune

Old walls of wood creak when air cools
Tree spoke to folks indoors a rustling lingo

Crisp lettuce on their plates and red meat
Perched in tree same bird sang as now

Pecan tree sole hero still grows
Slowly war and work fetched those folks away

Too bad house now gone to seed
In trashed rooms white devils hang out

Tending itself — a tree in majesty
Glued to gum, soda pop, the white mouth

Look again: no thought can be too high
Of whisper locked in white heart

Tell thought: still harder time ahead
Don't hold against them drift of old song

Coral Snake

I had been planting the sliced seed potatoes
When the snake started up from underfoot
And slithered across the gravel I stood on.

His beauty was not the point.
He was the kind that kills in a minute or two —
Chop off the finger he bit, or else.
But he was beautiful: alternating the black,
Red, and yellow rings more regular far, thick or thin,
Than wedding bands on a jeweller's ringstick.

He had come out of nowhere like evil.
He didn't care about me or want me.
I cared about him enough — it was fear.

Fear, not for me, no, but for him, the snake:
Long-trapped, an old horror breaks loose,
Later you say Alas, the snake was beautiful.
So I wonder what I can kill him with,
And notice in my hand the hoe; he isn't far,
Full stretch in his ringed ripples I see him
Slithering east of the two asparagus ferns.

I whop the hoe down and nail his head in the gravel
Between the chicken wire fence and a vegetable frame.
But he won't let go, I'm wrong, his free head
Rose over the quartz and flint pebbles;
Wild, the taut pure body, to be moving on and on.

Nothing to be done; if I shift the hoe
He'll streak through the chicken wire and I'll be
Cut off. I pressed harder on the hoe blade,
His tough coil resisted and the head
Wove a figure of eight in a pocket of air.

I didn't want it to be done, I didn't.
But how now to stop, considering his pursuits,
Easygoing as he is, pinheaded, slow to bite —

They say his tooth sits so far back
He needs to chew to do you in.

For there was more snake now in me than him.
I pushed the hoe blade harder down
And reached around the gate post for a stone.
That stone I eased
Beneath his tiny weaving head, taunting him,
Then reached around the post for a second stone.

When I looked again
The small black head with its yellow nape band
Was pointing up and the mouth, opening, closing,
Snapped at air to repel the blind force
Which held him down.

I could not do it, not to him, looking so
True to himself, making his wisdom tell,
It shot through me quicker than his poison would:
The glory of his form, delicate organism,
Not small any more, but raw now, and cleaving,
Right there, to the bare bone of creation.

And so I gripped the second stone but steadily
Thumped that telling head down flat
Against the surface of the first stone.
The broken body, I lifted it up and dropped it
Later into a vacant honey jar. The colours
Now have faded; having no pure alcohol,
I pickled the snake in half a pint of gin.

Nostalgia

What metaphor can bring back
What metaphor
Like nothing else can
Bring back the beautiful girls
For all the world
Like nymphs in pools
They spread their limbs
In long convertibles
And shook free their hair
Riding the highways for ever

Wild Flowers

Like voices
They never grew in water;
All began with nobody there to see.
A warmth helped; mud propelled them; early
The seeds rode in animal pelts across immense
Reeling distances, or
Were blown through light by the wind,
Like lovers.

When we were bush mice
They settled, ignored, in the cooling places;
Blood took heat,
Bees ate them, lizards and happily
Spiders liked them. Lodged in the fat of horses
They travelled. Tigers, and us,
Still tree hoppers, hardly felt what colours
Ringed by unearthly
Fragrances without names they had.

Far off the glittering libraries,
Vases of blown glass;
But look,
On roadsides they exist. Songs in our hands
They go along with us. A passion
Means us to pick them, so
Responding to early light we stop; then drive on home
To draw blankets back
And make our love while sensing them,
Their far fields, their darknesses.

Dirge for the Mistress of Screaming Animals

Woke in the night
Amazing silence
Somewhere moon

Filling my hide out —
Milk, a truth —
Drank from a mirror

No sound in street
All systems muted
No buzz, no roar

No shout or shooting
Icebox, even
Forgot to hum

Ah but I longed
Solo in silence
For breath dream-quickened

A rustle beside me
Flesh on linen
Longed for her

Her scraps of sleep talk
Name she'd murmur
Said she worked

As a lab assistant
Chicks and rats
React to her shots

I see her stand
At the lab door heeding
Quick rat chatter

Her charts record
Behaviour graphs
In sign and figure

Why, mistress of
Screaming animals
Nevermore babble

Of mutable habits
Skills crepuscular
Hiding and seeking

Snap your fingers
Clatter a dish
Play me your heart beat

Give me your long shot
Fathom my sorrow
With your lost love cry

Days of Heaven

Night rain beats down on the roof,
Hearing it
A flesh melts —

Shallow graves, crazy places
And morning comes,
Happiness, we make toast

Bivouac

Among the Polish Chassidim, perhaps among the Chassidim generally in Eastern Europe, it was prohibited to leave a book open in the village reading room. A sacred book, that is. Interfering forces might invade it, or escape from it.

A shadow might, otherwise, cross the open pages. The shadow might distort the features of a divinity which inhabited the pages, at once hidden and open. Or an expression on those features might run wild in the world, unmediated by any mind, the reader's, who sat there in his cloak being bothered by his fleas.

The world desired to be dulled. If not by the mind of this or that reader, with or without fleas, then by the clapping shut of the book. Otherwise the pneuma might break out and be at large, tigerishly among the furrowed desks, or hopping mad in the muddy or sunbaked little village streets.

The book had covers to shield its pages from mud or sunlight. Not even fingers had any title to cross the track of the word. The covers also existed to contain the scorching majesty of the word. At least, a risk was set aside. Who knows, the majesty might otherwise choose to spill out as idiocy and make havoc, or too much heaven, among the huts.

It was also an offence to place one open book on top of another open book. The charms of the pneuma were inviolable, transcendental.

The light shoots shadows into this room, across the pages of books and a few squares of Philippino reed carpet. Somehow I love it so. Outside, the trunk of an elm spells out a green shadow across blades of grass, the quiverings of which can only be detected if you take the time to watch, if you truly care, if you quiver a bit yourself. The grass blades tilt at an inexplicable mass of angles. Their tips ought to be points, but actually are bitten off, because every so often I try to mow the shadows down and the mower's cruciform blade rips across them. Underneath the mower's metal casing the momentarily unseen, as grass, suffers this.

No matter. A sheet of paper on the desk surface carries the print of the insect screen, a tight cross-hatching. This keeps the little winged demons out and holds a whiteness in. Nothing written contradicts the self-sufficiency of the word; its complex force, noted only in various proximate oscillations, disdained by the flea, unapparent in action, otherwise in hope, is a fiction so threatening that we devise our most dazzling footwork to pull a little fruit out of the teeth of disaster.

Here, too, on this bitter grass near dusk I saw the cicada come into being. First it had made its long journey up a perpendicular tunnel to the earth surface; the cicada itself had lubricated the tunnel with a juice it exuded through its protective pupa. Now, inside the bronze pupa, which was crisping, a general shiver began to happen. An infinitesimal foot prodded a hole in the pupa, then another foot. Gradually the head was coming out, then the body, forwards, but for twenty minutes it made a lunge, rested, lunged again. Its moment of emergence was so prolonged that it could hardly be seen emerging. The motive and the power behind this effort — barely imaginable — I felt them in my groin as a sensation between craving and fright, then in my throat as a taste, brandy and pepper.

Finally, mute and dull, an oval pellet had shrugged the pupa off. The pellet put a leg out, soon another leg. Its back was turning emerald, then golden emerald, with wings that lay flush with the pellet, exceedingly frail, then larger, unfurling into twin networks of golden emerald filigree tracery. And the head, with eyes, had woken up, was turning this way and that way; now the wings could move and lift. The cicada glowed as if dusted with a pollen out of which, for the sake of argument, the breath of a beyond conjectured the world's first agile anatomies. Pristine forest contracted to the volume of a singing bird's egg. A fiery drop of universe at the other end of a tunnel through time.

So I lay down on the grass and put an ear to it. I was expecting the wings to rustle and give off a melodious twang, faint as the last echo of a Jew's harp in an Egyptian burial chamber.

Then it simply wasn't there. From high up in an elm its first ancient cackle fizzed into the onset of dark.

A Carpenter Verbatim

More or less confident what I see is there
With no place else to go
Call a dog from the stoop anytime
Likely he'll trot across and look at you
You bet a word can be so spoken
It plumbs this thing or that action

Who's to say though what stuff escapes
When you pull up the string
There was this neat house I worked opposite
And people in it
A neat house to warm the new society

Someone shot
Brains and blood I tell you
Stuck in the shag carpet streaked walls
The people went on living there
Never cleaned up

Got the old lady to lower the rent
Two years (because because)
Till the lease ran out
Never took fright his ghost might show
Never shook out the chips of skullbone

Ate their food watching TV
What sort of people I don't know
What can have been biting him
The one
Who shot himself the hick
They near as likely killed

But your spiral staircase now
Looks so pretty
From the top
Hang a mirror from the beam or fit one
In the ceiling sheet rock

Someone going down could look right up and
Never see himself at all
For seeing it

Svatava's Dream

Twice changed, forty years
Different country, different person

There I was, again, you must
Have heard me tell

How when I was eleven, all
The books of this old writer, how

Eagerly I read them, mystic, yet
Only now, back, beyond the river

Was I aware how close I was to him,
And found my way down cobbled

Lanes, twisting
Into his pink museum

Found some friends, a man, a woman
Had made a painting of a house

It was pink and breathing, walls
Went out and in, windows

Pink, the air was flowing out and
In again, I heard the sounds

The city sounds, just as ever
They had been, just as ever

But they said the house was mine
Mine if I wanted the pink museum

Yet the painting was my house
Here, not there, stone, this

House I live in, mine, of stone
It hurt me so to choose, I could not

Tell whose pink house was there or here
To be mine if I wanted

Was it for me, the old museum
The writer's mystical pink

And me eleven, was the picture
Where I am, or in a renovated

Hradshin room, was this a time
When you breathe fast and double

A time in the flush of being
A house you make with breath

Go pink and everything
For you are torn

Far-From-Home Poem

A far-from-home poem
Foolish you can't put it together
The fingers tremble
A glistening cave in the guts
Fills with bats very eager for flight
Cries of children come from the sky
Little mouths everywhere open

It is not the place that calls like this
The place calls in its own fashion
With a smell of cedar smoke in early light
Transparent emerald

It calls with the buzzard
Seen above oaks and circling
As you lie in a hammock naked
It calls with the bodies of things
A little statue a Roman lamp a waterpot
You gathered up for they outlive you

Lake in the morning see fish
Flit through luminous shallows
Bird call cutting outline
On sky nothing but bird call
Nothing you can put a sense to

A clean sheet once in a while
Calls
And waking to enfold in your arms
A being who still dreams and kicks you
Says don't stop my dream

Not much of a roof as the sun
Hacks it into crinkles
And the rain calls
And the pipes that are stopped with roots
And the animals I mean wild ones

With curiously spelled names
Like you are for a while their neighbours
You dare to intrude

If only the snakes were more ferocious
If only the insects were worse
What a call you might hear
The terrible clamour of wings the orchestra of fangs
Snapping

As it is the bamboo just clicks
Clatters when the wind blows at moonrise
And the catbird calls in it
To the dog who is hungry
Mocking

The Turquoise

Somehow the memories fizzle out on us.
Large black eyes of people starving.
A snatch of music soon
Will be Merida, the mirrored bedroom, not
The pang felt there, but a fountain
Touches palm trees. Pang —

I forgot how perception had to be
Wrenched from its
Regular socket: the speech of folds, eyewhite
And snow the robe a woman wore,
Foreign liquor
The smell of a man at noon in his hammock.

Raw stuff: a crooked
Line of objects. Look, it is put
Straight like hair by distance.
The whole shadow of (our tune) your smile
Oozed first from
Repetition on a jukebox. Careless

Memory cooks
The kind of meal you
Gulp down, because the right place
Had shut, or the old prices are
Out of sight. Compulsion
Turns you still

Back to the same town: the flies
In children's eyes are blue, the drowned
Horse prongs the air still,
Silver hoof; never sensing wrong,
The deadly salesmen frisk again
With girls in the disco.

Swat a fly, scratch the wall
Of an ear with a toothpick: four, suddenly,
The grouped figurines
Loom huge from the desk angle,
And glow, clay Chupicuaro, bronze
Krishna, the wooden African —

As gods. To construct them
Ancestors broke through their skins,
Getting this far at least: the rock
Crystal coyote, stud him
With turquoise, let the orange fire
Be a tail like a beacon;

For the unseen escapes,
The remembered
Dominion cracks, falsifies
Desire and presence as they fly screaming
Before us, headdress and tail
Bushy, slashing backward in the dark.

A Forge in Darkness

They hadn't forgotten his name
Or whereabouts the forge was,
The brick oven, hot glow
Of charcoal, the hammer floats
Up, held in mid-air now, and
What beer the old man drank.

A heart isn't like that. A heart
Won't wait until the dark
Comes to cool things off a bit.
It works through the blinding
Noon heat, careless of sparks,
Of hoofs clipclopping uphill.

Boys came by. Owls looked on.
A horse tail flicked at bluebottles,
Under the canopy of this pecan.
This hill — part of the night then,
A slope, that's all, crested with a forge,
Like a wave flecked with red foam.

What a letdown for her, hitched
To that limping, fretful man,
The reek of sweat and charcoal on him —
And her arms could take a whole sky in,
Her thumbs govern long ships or fondle lambs,
Yet she slid from her wave and under him.

It was here, right here, where I came
To be living. She's gone, he's gone.
I cook chicken where the forge
Must have been. In the dark I
Pour out more wine to remember
The little old lives of them.

Taking a chance, I think
That's where she must have gone:
Into the artifice of not forgetting
A name and what went on,
When the boys watched and owls
Heard the hammer come down.

Postscript

'Jacob's Hat' is based on the mural by Delacroix in the church of St. Sulpice, Paris. 'Halicarnassian Ghost Dialogue' is about Herodotus. 'In Memory of Peter Szondi': the "beech wood" detail derives from the German context — *Buchstabe* = letter, and runes were originally made of beechwood sticks (*Buche* = beech). Buchenwald = Beech Wood. The scholar Peter Szondi was actually released from Auschwitz early in the 1940s while still in his teens, but the experience marked him for life. His suicide by drowning followed soon after that of his friend Paul Celan. 'Cabaret de la Canne, January 1855' is based on Alfred Delvau's report of an encounter with Gérard de Nerval (unbeknownst) shortly before his suicide. 'People in Kansas, 1910' elaborates on a postcard photograph, hence the postage stamp toward the end. I'm grateful to Sally Sullivan for letting me use her unpublished draft version of the 11th–12th century original as a basis for 'Shih-Ch'u's Magic Letter'.

I called the second of the two collections in this book *Apocrypha Texana* because the poems in it are anomalous in the frame of writing by native or settled Texans about their immense and varied habitat. Some poems allude to other parts of North America, but the terrain for many is Travis County, South Central Texas.

The preliterate idiom of 'Woden Dog' modulates from quasi-Old English through quasi-Black to a compound of Black and Western Apache English patois. It was a female voice I was hearing when I wrote the poems (Berlin, Winter 1978).